TUMBLED DRY

TUMBLED DRY

poems by
Charmaine Donovan

Lost Hills Books
Duluth, Minnesota

Tumbled Dry copyright 2011
by Charmaine Donovan.
All rights reserved.

This work may not be reproduced or transmitted, in whole or in part, without the written permission of the author.

Cover art: "Everlasting," mixed media by Sue Bowen
Cover design: Aaron Bosanko
Layout: Aaron Bosanko

Printed in the United States.

ISBN 10: 0-9798535-4-0
ISBN 13: 978-0-9798535-4-8

Lost Hills Books
PO Box 3054
Duluth, MN 55803
www.losthillsbks.com

for Jim—
your optimism carries both of us

ACKNOWLEDGMENTS:

My sincere thanks to the editors of the following publications in which some of these poems first appeared:

The Brainerd Daily Dispatch, County Lines, Differing Visions (a collaborative arts project), *Dust & Fire, Elegy for Jeanette, The Moccasin; Encore, NFSPS Prize Poems; From Ottertail and Thereabouts, Lake Country Journal, The Talking Stick, Twenty Poets Celebrate the Lake Country*. Poems forthcoming in *Her Voice*.

I extend my gratitude to the Five Wings Arts Council for their continued support. This book is the culmination of many classes, workshop, and conference experiences too numerous to list on this page. *This project was made possible by a grant provided by the Five Wings Arts Council with funds from the McKnight Foundation.*

With the guidance of Jill Breckenridge, this manuscript reached its final form. Her invaluable editorial experience and expertise is much appreciated.

Few books would be published if there were not willing publishers. Through an invitation extended by Bruce Henricksen, Lost Hills Books publisher, a lifelong goal and dream was ushered into reality. I will always value this first-time opportunity.

A special thanks to Michael Dennis Browne, my first poetry professor at the University of Minnesota; to the League of Minnesota Poets, especially the Heartland Poets chapter; to other Minnesota and nationally-known poets whose work I admire; to family and close friends for their support and dogged encouragement.

CONTENTS

I SYMPHONY OF IMAGES

Waterways 3
Spring Reflections in Fall 4
Snapshot of an October Afternoon 5
Equine Appetite 6
Falling into Winter 7
Cat Burglar 8
Xmas, The Missing Figure 9
Final Ascent.......................... 10
Georgia O'Keeffe: Symphony of Images 11

II TUMBLED DRY

Heavenly Bodies 15
Reflections........................... 16
Strip Poker........................... 17
Coffee Shop Girl Reinvents Woman ... 18
Super Valu 19
Benchmark Season: Summer '67....... 20
Teens and Mail A-Go-Go 21
Alan on the Lam 22
Closeted Memories.................... 23
Porthole to the Future 24
Small-Town Yield..................... 25
Spaced Out: July 20, 1969............. 26
Tumbled Dry......................... 27

III RAINY RECOLLECTIONS

Avenues of Sleep...................... 31
Road Doctor & Wildflower............ 33
Goodbye Aftermath 34
When Rain Returns 35
Rainy Recollections 36
Welcoming the Storm................. 37
Best Friends Shine On 38
Thwarted by the Thinness of Paper 39
Trapdoor of Time 40
Fossil Friendship 41

IV KEEPER OF GOOD THINGS

Her Lipstick Still on the Cup 45
Snow Games 47
Phantom Pet 48
The Great Lake Superior's Reign....... 49
Lesson under Glass 51
Mindless Clutter of Skyjunk 52
We Talk Germs in Alateen Group 53
Thinking of Crookston 54
Keeper of Every Good Thing 56
Deliberate Day 57

V CAST ON / CAST OFF

Rodin's The Thinker (1880) 61
Cast On / Cast Off 62
Bicycling Highway 65................. 63
Rendered Peachless................... 64
Tomato Speculation 65
Bananamania 66
Dancer Eyes......................... 67
Birthplace of a Poet 68

TUMBLED DRY

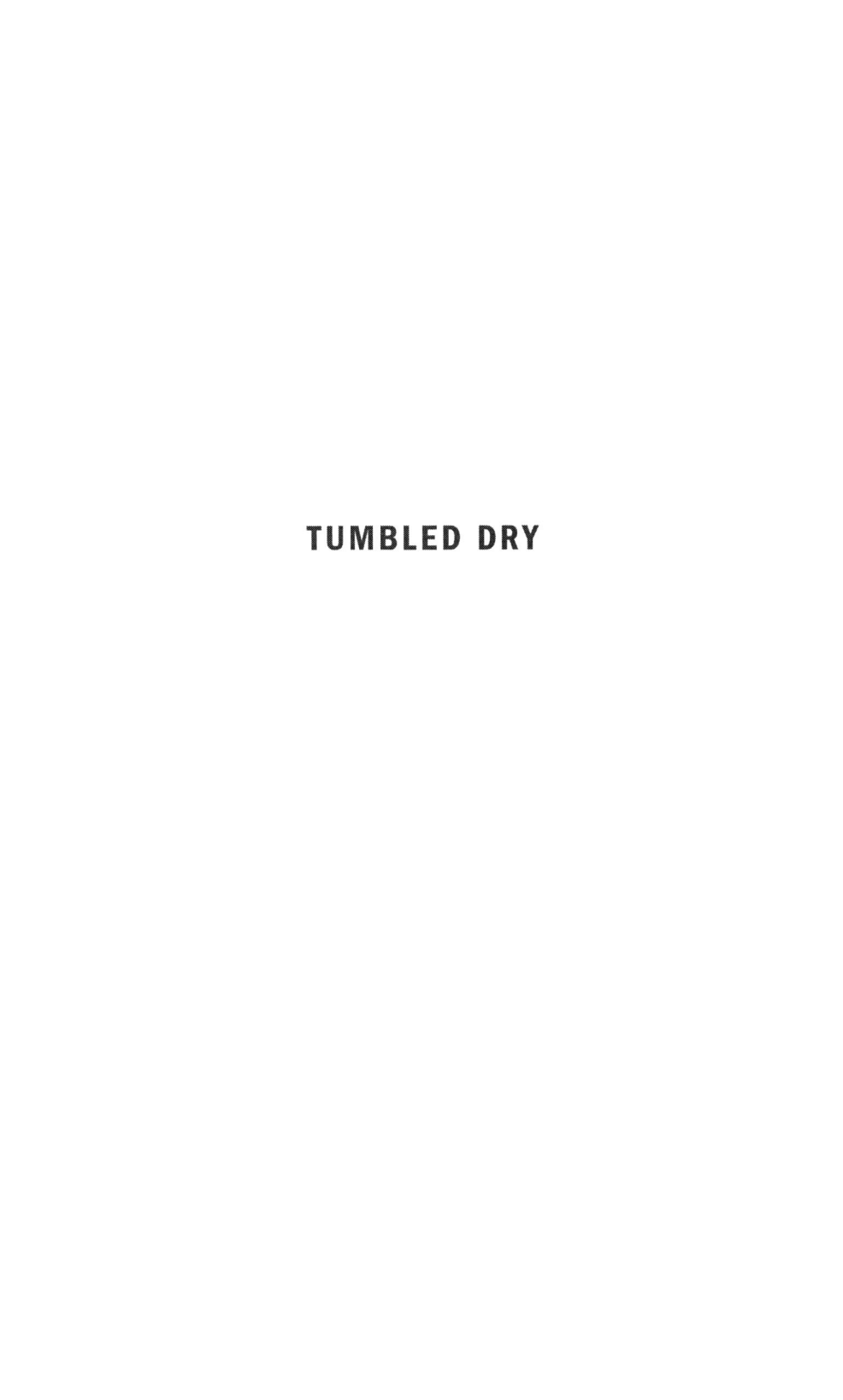

*The eye is the lamp of the body. If your eyes are good,
your whole body will be full of light. But if your eyes are bad,
your whole body will be full of darkness.*

Matthew 6:22-23

I SYMPHONY OF IMAGES

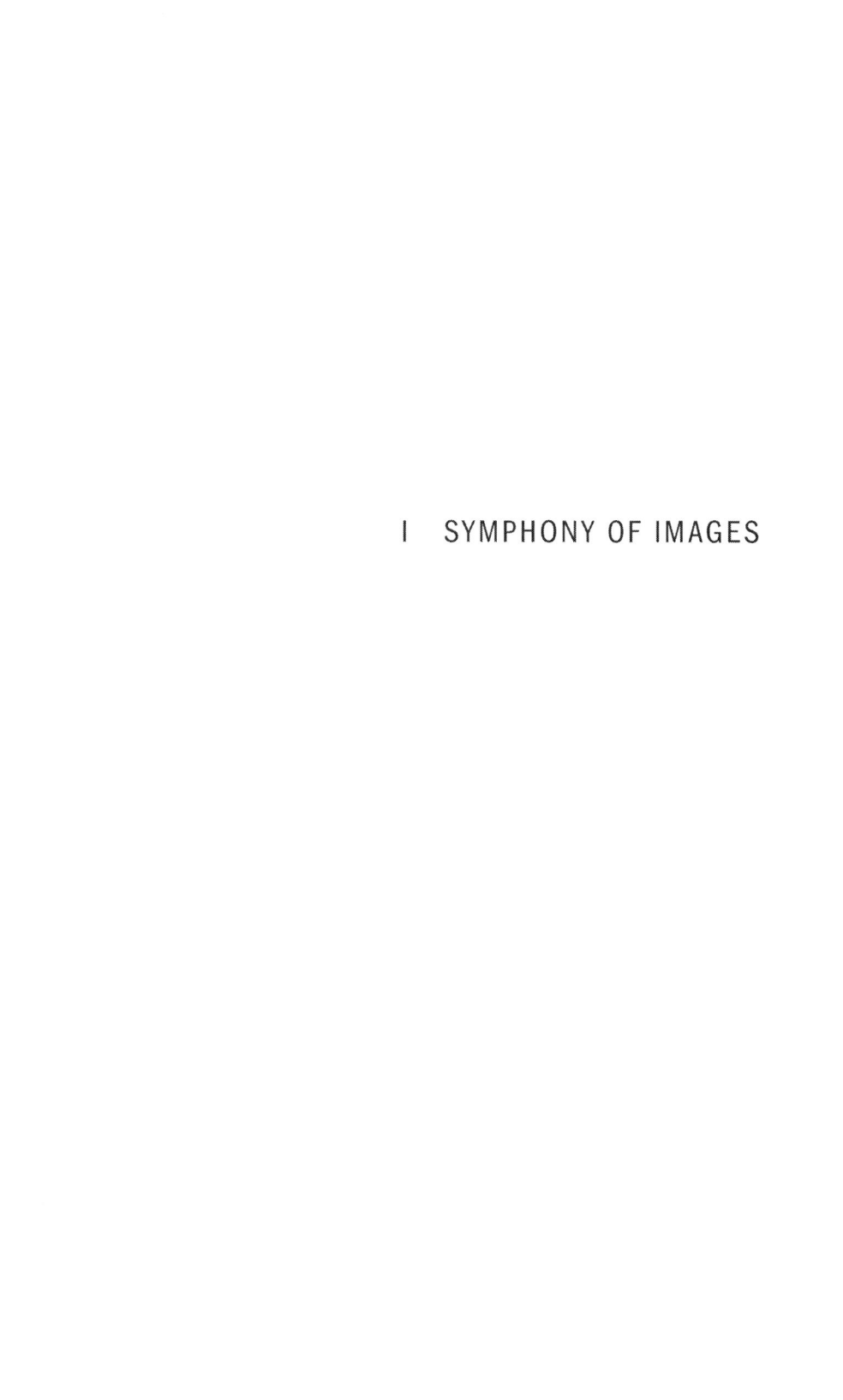

WATERWAYS

Sunday is a silver day,
not like yesterday's wet pewter.
Today the lake glows
like a new quarter.
We launch the boat,
churn silver into white waves.
Above the motor's murmur,
our thoughts turn liquid, weedless,
untangling in smooth silence.

Passing between buoys
under a wooden bridge
and inching through the bay,
we smile and wave
at strangers in swimming suits,
boaters whose minds unwind
thread held on spools
by tension, now released.
Our eyes catch the statue stillness
of blue heron, yellow glint
of water lilies blooming among green pads,
a mud turtle's orange belly flop
heading from bank to bottom.

We slow ourselves, floating,
in our womb-memory of suspension,
the warmth of our mother's heat
beating like the sun,
that vague sound of her words,
balm to our sloshing spirits
destined for an unexpected shore.

SPRING REFLECTIONS IN FALL

It can't be fall in Minnesota.
(Ripe time to shed
summer's sizzle
and become bare as bones.)

Fall hasn't traced
a bold transforming face
in vague reflections of this lake
that still blooms spring.
Wiggly lines of birch blend,
leaves bend, a swirl of paisley cloud
our eyes can walk upon.

In this secluded pool
fish fins stir cool liquid quietly.
Monet's fiery water lilies float
on garden-branded memory.

Our eyes forget known fact
of cool, crisp days
that darken sooner,
slipping from the sun
to hide behind
a glazed and frosty moon.

Our eyes behold
burst blossoms,
raspberry-sweet,
from puckered buds of green.
Tied to branches,
garlands in a May Day dance
sway invitation to be touched
and held aloft, to twist and turn
in variegated steps,
binding braided centerpost
to the foreverness of spring.

It can't be fall in Minnesota
while this lake's soul
reflects blurry breezes
of a blossoming spring.

SNAPSHOT OF AN OCTOBER AFTERNOON

Plumes of trees
feather a humped horizon.
From the road
gray remnants of a house
sag—full of ghosts
and other restless things.
Boarded windows turn
glassy eyes inward,
their lids closed
against outside storms.

The fiery heat of woods
looms ready to lick
an abandoned dwelling
into a funeral pyre.
Yet feeble yellow grassland
on the verge of winter somnolence
holds this home
in its soft palm,
pillow for an old dreamer
knee deep in sleep.

EQUINE APPETITE

Horse instinct is to graze, and graze they will
as nimble lips keep nibbling apropos
until their appetite consumes its fill.

Beneath low bushes, over a distant hill,
around field fence posts, near the patio;
horse instinct is to graze, and graze they will

regardless of inclement weather, chill.
They'll forage during thunderstorms, in snow,
until their appetite consumes its fill.

Surprisingly, they'll sometimes stand stock-still
like statues cued to reach where grasses grow.
Horse instinct is to graze, and graze they will.

While dreaming, can illusive fields fulfill
an eager urge to mosey to and fro
until their appetite consumes its fill?

Impossible to understand the thrill
of eating almost endlessly, although
horse instinct is to graze, and graze they will
until their appetite consumes its fill.

FALLING INTO WINTER

The gloom of dawn has burned off
and the sky lights up like a bright lake.
Puddles from yesterday's rain punctuate
hollows on the pavement and lawn.

The leaves are turning:
a maple's ignited blaze contrasts
the low yellow flame of birch nearby,
oaks twisting from green to ruddy.
As days shorten, they remind us

of the impending darkness of winter.
Thank goodness for the dancing snow!
How lavishly a white accumulation of flakes
drape their crystalline sparkle
on windows, fence posts, and mailboxes.

This crunch underfoot heralds a new iciness
as our breath billows before us—
and we know we are alive,
wrapped in the warmth of our layered lives.

CAT BURGLAR

He drifted to our doorstep in a storm
of snow, as though he were a piece of night
and blazing light. A contradiction formed
in shadowed seas of snow festooned with white.
He hid beneath our stoop until he heard
slight sounds of footsteps scrape the kitchen floor.
He leapt upon the porch, then scratched, assured
that someone would acknowledge, not ignore
these sneaky sounds. Bright light beamed on his face:
its jester black and white, so comical!
Round eyes like headlights beamed, and yet embraced
my own. His plea was purely animal.
   Inside my skin a furry mammal stirred.
   I slid the door—he padded in, he purred.

XMAS, THE MISSING FIGURE

A brown bag-packaged crèche
rattles an unwrapped discovery:
the manger-baby is missing from the scene.

Gently shaking the stable for noise
while it's crooked under an arm,
my fingers dig into a musty corner,
probe the hollow scrapes, until I hold
within the palm of my hand,
a half-swaddled plastic Christ,
his arms open
in a universal blessing to all.

I reason my infant faith
unready for the grown man,
an empty tomb,
yet a seasonable distance away.
I carefully glue Jesus
back into his birthplace.

FINAL ASCENT

Hey look, don't worry about me too much.
Last words radio-telephoned to pregnant wife
by Rob Hall, climber who died in a blizzard
on Mount Everest, May 11, 1996

Descending
from 29,028 feet
for the fifth time,
feeling as invincible
as any warrior will,
—500 feet below the peak—
he is shaken by frozen fists
of an abominable blizzard
until terror dips away in rounded fluff.

In a place where fear ceases to divide,
where worry is no longer a common denominator,
this climber crouches in the cloaking calm of death.

Beyond labored breath, beyond white winds of lethal
cold, a glaring light hotter than any he has known, penetrates
like a piton, digs into the stone of his spirit, lifts him onto flesh-
less shoulders, far safer than any he had imagined. From here he
is carried higher, to another summit farther than every sky where
he can see his frozen body crouched solid in snow, small and useless.

GEORGIA O'KEEFFE: SYMPHONY OF IMAGES

*In her canvases each color almost regains the fun
it must have had within itself on forming the first rainbow.*
  -Charles Demuth, artist

My art blossomed with burgeoning flowers—
evolved to blocky buildings, surreal scenes.
I scouted Southwest's mesa and desert
tooling my Model A for covered bones.
I camped in sand—sans husband, city life—
to paint God's Pedernal bent in music.

Colors danced onto canvas like music:
tympani drumrolls, pulse-pump of flowers
framed larger than camera-recorded life.
I wanted to contain these footloose scenes,
relish rare moments, resonating bones.
I sifted bland truths entombed in desert

dunes, begged oaths from smooth skies to not desert
pearl clouds, nor ever overwhelm music:
blues sung through eye sockets, skulls of dried bones.
Evening stars like sheriff badges, flowers
loosed at sunset will not arrest forged scenes
concocted here in this forever-life.

Leaves, feathers, shells—organic stand-still life
I brushstroked into being. My desert,
a horse, unbridled, chock full of wild scenes;
jammed notes gritty with duststorm music,
tempered with sun, tough as yucca flowers.
I drew clues from the marrow of old bones.

Skulls, pelvises viewed at odd angles, bones
became another way to look at life.
More real than my gargantuan flowers,
fragile poppies, victims in bronze desert
sun. They withered, frightfully, like music
melting, notes died off at a crime-filled scene.

Sky Above Clouds, an aptly final scene.
No longer any need to dwell on bones.
Pure melody, symphonic song, music

on high, untouched by vagaries of life.
Beyond, picture a celestial desert
where bouquets sing on: forever flowers.

Uniquely painted scenes portray stark life
down to bare bones. My own sultry desert
songs: music strengthening souls and flowers.

II TUMBLED DRY

HEAVENLY BODIES

We were not cheap tricks
as we walked the streets.
While our bodies bloomed
in matching flowered shirts,
we poured ourselves into rear-
hugging stovepipe pants.
The rubber toes of our new bumper
tennies shined like childhood patent leather.

We were hipless, girlfriends
halfway through our teens,
our dolls ditched for real action.
Dark-haired Barbies on the lookout
for their faceless, groovy Kens.

We walked the sidewalks
while sunshine and moonbeams
tracked our aimless route.
We traipsed through town,
wore our youth like tiaras
on the glistening hair of beauty queens.

Main Street was our runway.
Our thoughts circled like our walks,
as familiar and repetitive as lyrics
to every favorite Beatles' song.
Up and down streets,
hitchhiking on highways,
we carried our dreams
on our backs like magic carpets.
They kept us warm on cold nights
when coats were thin

and no one seemed to notice
how we twinkled,
how this orbit was meant
to steer us from that lukewarm town,
a town whose gravity
held our bodies earthbound,
kept us from melting the stars.

REFLECTIONS

I stand in my bathroom before the mirror,
its stark silvery image reflecting my age.

I complete my cleansing regimen,
pat dark circles and wrinkles with cover-up,

think of Patty Leino as I brush my teeth.
I see us shivering in our white gym suits

outside on the football field (it becomes
the track field after football season).

The gym suits cover our ironing board busts, fabric
flat against the hope of what we wish we had.

We're in seventh grade and only Rhonda Boulder
has boobs and wears bras with cups. We're still wishing.

We've just completed the hurdles, a fright, we're sure,
in our $32 gym suits, the bloomers flashing under shorts.

Our legs have bloody scrapes from the jumps we missed.
Patty is Finn, blonde, white-skinned and tall.

She is diabetic, I don't know why I think of that.
We stand shaking, fatigued, on the track field

in our white regulation tennis shoes. It's a dreary day.
We're chagrined by the evidence of our clumsiness.

Patty's bent forward, and I tower over her for once.
I notice the curl of her eyelashes, a wood tick among them.

I try not to talk, not to think of that bug sucking her blood,
but it's as impossible as not thinking about boys. So I tell her

she has a tick on her left eyelid, hidden among her lashes.
She pulls, flicking it off like a memory into the grass.

STRIP POKER

Holding cards in our hands, while trying to cover naked parts of ourselves with less-naked parts of ourselves, wasn't easy. Nor was it a cinch deciding which cards to throw away while giggling our girly self-conscious heads off in the playhouse or windowless garage. We never got brave enough to play the game with boys, although since males are very visual, strip poker was probably invented by them. We sat around drinking Coke or Pepsi, used the empty cans as ashtrays while we smoked cigarettes stolen from our parents or older siblings. If we couldn't get ahold of real tobacco, we lit up reed-like sticks we pulled from a nearby swamp. We sat on our t-shirts huddled in our modesty, shoulders hunched over barely budding breasts, our legs pulled close, ankles crossed near triangles starting to sprout hair. We wanted to be able to say that we had done more than play Spin the Bottle. We wanted junior high boys to turn red when they thought of us in our bras and panties, then turn even redder when they pictured us without them.

COFFEE SHOP GIRL REINVENTS WOMAN

She enters her Metallic Phase:
     gold lamé dresses
     mirror-lensed shades
     silver threads
     bronze purse-on-a-string
Clunky copper platforms
stretch her neck three inches longer
(like mushroom-eating Alice
     in her la-la Wonderland)
Brass gong earrings announce her arrival

Launched into the Space Age:
     moon-walking
     knee-deep in marshmallow boots
     sausage-tight in jumpsuit Lycra
        elbows splashed with electric gloves
        hairdo defies gravity
She is beamed into realms beyond probability

Swirl-girl in short, sequined float dress
held up on legs smooth & curvy as dowels
     skin sealed in stardust
        lips like a full, cloud-cluttered moon
        eyelids darkened into black holes
Through folds of her shimmering shift
gleam outlines of her galactic figure

A Planetary Woman sculpted in particles of time

SUPER VALU

Of course I dressed up when I went with my mother to the biggest grocery store in town. I was going to be in public, I was going to be seen. I dressed up like every teenager too young to drive who had nowhere to go. I pawed through my wardrobe like a model on her way to walk the red carpet. My makeup was impeccable—every Twiggy bottom lash painted on, the top ones mascaraed to the nth degree, lipstick pale pink or white, giving lips a slightly bluish hue. Mom would tell me to hurry up, but she always waited. This time I walked down the stairs in my white hip-huggers, wearing red, white and blue platforms, and a red and white striped sailor top. I could see that she approved, though she had said the wide legs were a bit over-the-top. What did she know? She was my mom. At the store, while at the check-out counter, she dug in her purse for pennies. I rolled my eyes at the grocery bagger, a junior, who carried the sacks to our car. "Thank you," I called over my shoulder while opening the passenger door. "You're welcome, ma'am," he said. Over and over I replayed his three-word reply. Was he mocking me? Did he ignore me and thank only my mother? Was he saying, "Hey, I see you girly-girl, but I have orders to say 'ma'am' and 'sir' to all the customers." When I saw him wrestle on the mats that winter, his sweaty body in maroon tights, I imagined myself washing his uniform by hand, scrubbing the crotch extra good.

BENCHMARK SEASON: SUMMER '67

Summer of the Beatles' *When I'm Sixty-Four*—
I know because of that first kiss near the beach
after a boy sang the lyrics "Will you still need me,
will you still feed me..." as I listened from the green bench
dressed in a Twiggy-inspired, hand-sewn geometric shift.
My metal-mouthed smile bright as tinfoil,
a telltale sign of youth, cancelled out
the sophistication of smoking and bleached blonde hair.

When Top Forty songs finally lost their appeal,
we lay underneath the bench, shaded.
Our bodies indented smooth soft sand,
soaked in the heat of a July sun. Silent moments
crescendoed to watching a crescent moon
through cracks in the slats, holding gritty hands,
and finally that one perfect kiss, lips to lips,
soft and wet, tasting of spearmint and wonder.

TEENS AND MAIL A-GO-GO

Eager to listen to live rock bands,
we descended a steep stairway
underground into that windowless basement
beneath the post office on Main Street.
We paid our babysitting and dishwashing dollars,
had our hands stamped by adult chaperones
who leaned close to see if they could smell
booze on our under-aged breath.

The band and bathrooms were at the far end
of this narrow cavernous room
with folding chairs placed strategically
along the cement-block walled perimeter.
An unlikely room to captivate youth,
transformed by the heat of bodies
in motion, strobe lights, and loud music.

On Friday nights after hours in the post office
letters boogalooed in their numbered boxes,
matched our watusi moves to *Wipeout*.
How many packages lost their stamps
sweating to the lyrics of *Purple Haze*
or grooving to Iron Butterfly's
psychedelic *In-A-Godda-Da-Vida*?
How many envelope tongues tangled
while paired-up in a slow-dance
to *House of the Rising Sun*?

ALAN ON THE LAM

Following in your mother's drunken footsteps,
on pills and Mad Dog, a formula you thought
far better than her vodka, I met a hung-over you
on a green bench at the Fourth Street Park.
The next night I watched as you and your friends
lit matches along the avenue, flung jackknives
into the grass in a game of Stretch.
I wanted to save you like I wanted to rescue
any featherless bird fallen from its nest,
or a turtle too slow to dodge tire treads.
Fascinated by the embers of your being, I reached out,
warming, then singeing the tips of my fingers.
I sputtered, burned by the folly of my curiosity.

We rolled in leaves, our pressing hugs
and tongue-twisted kisses all we could steal
when neither one of us had anywhere to go.
But I went home to my safe little town
while you fell victim to the needle;
a heroin overdose I was told.
Too late I learned you were underground, dead;
another city boy careened out-of-control.
How I longed to twist my fingernail-bitten fingers
through your blonde, scraggly hair,
see the scant, darker hair growing
above your upper lip, kiss those cold,
pouty lips, gray as a winter sky.

CLOSETED MEMORIES

Visit to a friend's attic:
hangers of vintage clothes,
slack eras of shoes beneath.
Pea coats & Nehru jackets,
paisley dresses, vinyl skirts.
One, Summer in the City,
Michelle, late 60s-ish tunes.
Red, white & blue platform shoes,
hip-huggers, bellbottoms,
England Swings, Petula Clark,
The Mamas & The Papas.

Rollers the size of orange juice cans,
ironed hair, *Summer Blonde* hair dye.
The advent of *Boon's Farm, Ripple
& Bali Hai* wines. The advent of puberty.
High school dress codes:
boys wear belts, no jeans allowed;
girls dress & look like Barbie dolls.

Vietnam. Body counts & massacres.
Free love, bra waving, draft card burning.
1970 graduation, class song:
Bridge Over Troubled Waters.
Later 70s: sit-ins, demonstrations,
Kent State, students die;
soldiers die, Janis Joplin &
Purple Haze Jimi Hendrix die.
California's Haight-Ashbury,
The Electric Kool-Aid Acid Test,
Timothy Leary, LSD & PCP.

Hot pants, Frye boots,
GunneSax, shawls, *Earth* shoes,
granny square vests, halter tops,
bandana headbands & tie-dyed t-shirts.
Peace & love, hippy beads, hashish.
An avalanche of memories,
a Vesuvius tangle of clothes
Happy Together again.

PORTHOLE TO THE FUTURE

Sometimes sitting in the Laundromat,
my behind conformed to the hard plastic chair,
I look up from my ragged *Glamour* magazine
and peer intently into the large porthole—
a dryer's Plexiglass front, damp with washing,
and see past my reflection to the other side
where the low hum of a cruise ship's engines
pushes the prow through warm waves
while I stand naked in my stateroom, calm and dry.
I am grown, my body as smooth and hour-glassed
as Barbie's. I turn toward the shiny-sheeted bed
where a broad-chested Tarzan awaits me.
Eyeing my curves, he reaches to hold me,
and when I turn to him, I turn toward his love
like a sun whose blistering rays I have only imagined.

SMALL-TOWN YIELD

When you sprout from small town seed to weed, escape for years to The City, then return again—memory stirs. Inspired by the sight of landmarks scattered along a zigzag path toward adulthood, old scenes swirl like paisley in a sky filled with solid colors. This mixed bag, so full of farce and panic, was once upon a time discarded as childish, later lost in a hullabaloo of daily life. Now it looms large in an overactive mind stimulated by familiar sights. Some leftover images, though ragged and faded to almost invisible, still hover like ghosts from a gallery of scenes curled on the cutting floor.

Driving a road whose asphalt your teenaged tires knew intimately—every bump and curve, the contour of each corner, each ditch you avoided most of the time (except during a few sudden snowstorms), you see in the gloom of morning: Noah's house. Who knows? He may still live in that old gray wreck of a thing standing atop a hill.

You retread the scene when a carload of partygoers dropped him off there. Before you had time to wave good-bye, out the door he flew, ass-backwards, hands raised to defend his body against his mother's broom. A huge embarrassment, an incident no one mentioned unless flat-out drunk. What could you say? You were all out past curfew. You giggled nervously because who knew what sort of cockeyed scene you might run into once you'd reached home.

SPACED OUT: JULY 20, 1969

As families sit mesmerized
by blurry images flashing
on gray TV screens,
I take my own moonwalk
through the neighborhood.
High on drugs, earth has vanished.
Everything is alien
in this new glow of hallucination.

Streetlights interrogate asphalt,
squeeze pebbles of truth from tar.
Drawn like a bug into light's orbit,
I confess my doubt in God,
stammer how I've stolen dimes
from Mom's leather purse,
sob star tears for lying about it.

Drawn away from moonbeams,
I enter the noisy terrain of trees
whose backs bend in limbo dances
as wind-music carries me skyward.
I can walk—forever weightless—
on marshmallow boots,
claim clouds as acquaintances,
eat the cheese that moons are made of.
I can swallow this spaceship capsule
of a flower-child generation
                        and fly.

I am sixteen.   I blast off.   I fly.

TUMBLED DRY

While watching The Lawrence Welk Show
our parents called us *wet behind the ears*

as though we had a condition to be cured,
smoked to smithereens, or hung out to dry.

But, we teenagers were old enough
to know better and too young to care.

Whether the backs of our ears were dry
or not, we dared to tumble carelessly,

rough edges chipped off like agates
within a barrel, or daredevils who slid

down Niagara Falls on a whim. Scratched
and bruised, we usually survived the plunge.

Dryness may have implied a certain oldness,
bones creaking with old-school authority,

a Hee Haw humor we couldn't swallow,
spit out before its redneck reckoning set in.

Billy Graham's drive to save our souls
couldn't save us from the persuasive draw

of the draft, free-love, and mind-blowing drugs.
Tune in, turn on, drop out was our motto—

champagne music and TV bubbles were unreal
compared to acid rock, electrified wine, or keg beer.

We got lucky and had a second chance
to tumble dry, grab hold like drowning

victims seize lifelines, pay a quarter or more,
for what once cost a dime at the Laundromat.

III RAINY RECOLLECTIONS

AVENUES OF SLEEP

Remember me. I am your icon woman.
Anointed one to sink your thoughts into,
fantasize with and about, twirl around in circles
of your undanced do-si-dos.
Now, married to another,
you lasso me in a wagon train
of dreams. Thick-hipped & silent
you hook thumbs through belt loops,
cowboy-style, throw back your head,
snicker away years, blow into wispy hair,
taste my ear, arouse me as ever before.
Yawning behind us, fields of our disbelief
are hovered over by birds we watched together;
now they become vultures waiting for
our carcasses to cool.

. We are light-years apart,
our fate forever entangled
in a lopsided skein of duplicity, so complicated
these knots must be cut apart, never untied.
Like tourniquets, strands hold us together,
never bleed or pardon us from the years
we shared.

On avenues of sleep, you visit regularly
bent on reminding me of the youthfulness
of my misgivings. A wildflower,
I was challenged by rocky terrain,
ready to blare my trumpet dandelion dance
in sidewalk cracks, ready to believe
that sun and rain would smooth
deep gullies of indecision. I was wrong.
Today I weep for my mistake
like I cry for all the stolen children,
their pictures plastered on walls & milk cartons,
lives reduced to two-dimensional black-&-white.

I weep for all the buffet sunsets set before me,
bountiful banquets splashed with periwinkle,

fuchsia I forget to feed upon,
too tied up in the saran wrap of living
to catch glimpses of the primordial burning
of the sun, its heat a balm reminder
of all that came before...

...and will come after too.
I have become wrinkled with wisdom,
something you will never have to remember
about me.

Mired in our youth, strangled buds of an
exotic flower
dried into perpetual potpourri
only my dreams can smell.
In this horizontal state, our odd,
yet strangely satisfying reunions
will always remain safe
within my sleep.

ROAD DOCTOR & WILDFLOWER

You knew me   like you knew   machines
    engine   to take apart   put together
    parts   to fiddle with   greasy
    slick fun   for fidgety hands
Like so much love   ours   idled to a stop
    mechanics   being   only part
of beauty   more than   metal deep

Your dreams   rose   from junk heaps
    used parts   of disaster
        accidents
    stray   uninjured pieces
  collections   sorted   stacked
welded   into a steering machine

A road doctor   speed-demon
   instinctive   well-lubricated   motor-man
     primed   pumped   full of horsepower
  ignited   a piston   struck spark

You found me   at a roadside   stop
    in a field   of clover
whose perfume   danced   peculiar
    with exhaust   fumes
    hot rubber   on blustery days

Celebrating   from   the bucket seat
    you braked   for sweet softness
  curved upholstery   unfamiliar   female parts
Up close   you could not   rearrange
   limbs   waist   even face
    into   a well-oiled   engine
  nor make flesh   tremble   into life
    under   your nimble   fingers

We said   our goodbyes   in your truck
blades slashed   back and forth   on glass
  every   rain-streaked word   rusted
Ejecting   fuel   you   didn't know
  you'd need   to make   your motor run
    liquid love   whose   special charm
seeped out   like gasoline   onto grass

GOODBYE AFTERMATH

You are out there somewhere.
I see you glare at the spikes on your ceiling
grinding your teeth into questions I will never answer.
That night in the car, its shoulders in rain,
we passed a piece of metal back and forth,
symbol for hearts we could lend, never give away.
Even the glove compartment burst open,
filled with a discord of meaning.

When I spoke, you became stupid with anger.
Your ears only translated what you wanted to hear.
And now your piano will play for you:
its notes those words you let your fingers speak.

I'm not your woman anymore.
The path to your door is strewn with traps
that are yours and should be.
Your door has no knob. Let it.
The home we made for each other was an argument
belied by all the false starts we brought to it.
Yet if all the wrong reasons were piled together,
they must amount to something,
much as salvage bears a price.

Today I will go a round with you in my mind
for the old times that do not bury themselves easily.
I will talk to my cacti that will let me
pour out the slough which means goodbye;
spiny as these lives asking nothing,
that grow green in spite of a drought.

WHEN RAIN RETURNS

Grief mimics the suddenness of storms.

I hear water glisten.
I hear what is left after thunder.
I hear what has formed in clouds, and now,
unable to contain itself a fraction longer—
the bucket tips, drops fall, and splash everywhere.

I hear how clean the sound breaks,
arrows through dry air, and lands,
drumming distinct tones on different surfaces;
the dream dance of natives thrumming messages.
I hear what water cannot wash away.

I smell rain, dank strands of hair
dripping with liquid, teardrops
transparent as glass, the earthy odor
rising out of ground to meet air,
a deep throb, a sobbing scent.

I feel dots of damp cold,
the piercing, pressing drops
catch me as I run from cover to cover.
I think I can make it, eyes full of water,
drenched in a spontaneity of sky.

I see a sudden shatter of lightning,
the way brightness flickers,
jagged-edged, a rippling reptile
this electricity: its snarled tongue
straightens, ready to land and maim.

Rain returns. Invisible slashes pierce,
seek the hidden marrow of bones.
Like the labor of a false birth,
when this storm subsides
it leaves nothing to hold.

RAINY RECOLLECTIONS

I listen for his sole-scrapes on my stoop.
Waiting, quiet as a lynx stalking her prey,
my ears perk at the telephone's shrill ring,
mute today. His car, its black-tread wheels
could crunch onto the driveway all-of-a-sudden,
whoosh—cause the flat beats of my heart to leap
in peaks and valleys of unclimbed anticipation.

Half-awake, I hear branches scratch the siding
of this shriveled house, hear his big-hand knock
against my door. Warped wood quakes under his knuckle.
I sit up in disbelief until his voice thunders my name,
a sound that surfs on sheets of wet wind,
then trembles a raindrop dance onto my shoulders
where it rests, a drizzle of yarn twisted into soggy comfort.

 Drowsed, the damp smell of his familiar personhood
drifts into my realm of possibility: Brut aftershave,
Dial soap and a hint of peppermint. Leather jacket sleek
with rain, pointed collar raised around his skinny neck,
blonde hair zigzag-parted, misty-wet strands darkened.
In off-white chinos, his loafers are filled with dimes
whose Mercury heads he always said looked like mine.

He must have let himself in, beyond trapdoors of time,
to dwell in the squall of my turbulent sleep.
He conjures up swells of memory, stirring storms
as slippery and unsettled as this dream; real as clouds drifting
overhead, lost without a final destination, a resting place.
I, who since his death, wince in the wake sunshine,

will turn over the torrent of his passing. I will hang
out the water-logged recollection of him, to dry
on the splintered deck of my rudderless life.

WELCOMING THE STORM

There is no storm like the one raging within.

When my baby sister turns thirty-three,
I want to tell her to expect a whopping snowstorm
weathermen do-si-do in lukewarm forecasts.

I expect hungry horses pawing at stall doors,
black cat shadow-rubs against boot ankles.
If only she could see each white flake as a future
waiting blankly for sculpts and scrawls.

On January 12th my sister turns thirty-three.
She yawns as though today were
as unremarkable as yesterday.

She doesn't see snow coming,
prefers the backside of shaded windows
rather than squeaky-clean sunlight
lavish before a soon-to-be overcast day.

In the evening I call to sing her annual tune.
She's asleep, is supposed to call later.
No phone rings with her voice.

When my sister turns thirty-three,
I remember the smell of summer
like fresh snow, but don't rub it in;

I let its truth penetrate like sunburn, frostbite,
and never think of how young
a subtraction of fifteen years feels.

How an erasure could snatch my middle age—
turn it into something ready to dread,
or look forward to. Instead, I

peer out into a crystal-ball night
and predict a fresh future, snowy with wisdom
that falls from dark skies, storms.

BEST FRIENDS SHINE ON

Caught up   in earth's crafty rotation   time
has twirled by   without a hint   of movement
or hesitation   through space   invisible as air.
My head turns back   over a shouldered view
where I wonder   how   we invented games
that made you shine. My bulb dimmed   at second best.

Your cowgirl friends   crap slinging days
filled you full   of tough stuff   hay had to be hauled
life no longer   thought about   on hills   at 5 a.m.
with cocoa   in cold hands. Its steam   escaped us
like those ideas   we never moved   our lips   to speak.

My days   filled with drinks   mind-bending drugs
where truth & lies   melted   into a strange circus
where I was   the masked clown   encircled
in an arena   of laughter   inescapable as a noose.

Our lives   on separate islands   distant
counties   within the state   keep us apart.
While fingers   tap   familiar keys
at different desks   with wireless mice.

We share   a common cadence   in language.
You tend to business   gladly   create pages
that make   job seekers   shine
while I   dust off   my words
unshelve   & polish them   until   they glow
with sunshine   brighter than   hundred watt bulbs.

THWARTED BY THE THINNESS OF PAPER

She's melted into the mainstream,
patterning herself after the current motif,
blending into repetition like perfectly hung wallpaper.

She's taken back her words, unpublished them
from the ironed-on flatness of paper.
She's restored their three-dimensional reality
which had evaporated into a slim lie.

Now I, who could merely expose
write poetry, while she, who could
create and compose, types resumés.

TRAPDOOR OF TIME

> *I'm on my way out...*
> Words spoken by Jeanette Hinds
> less than a week before her death.

The time comes. We step onto the square
in front of our feet, outlined with the black
of certainty. There is no longer another path,
a different way to walk. We have tried other routes
and we sense some pathways too arduous for us now.

So we step onto that square of old age
beckoning before us, knowing the hinges are fragile,
that they will bear our weight
for just so long, then the metal will give way
and the boards beneath our feet splinter. We fall.

Our arms cling to the edges for a while,
hold bodies above the unknowable
as our feet dangle into darkness.
While suspended, we smell the dust of disturbed livestock,
a herd milling, hear the distressed sound of the displaced

like your childhood memory in the barn,
when play turned to terror
while you clung to the sides of the hay mow chute
screaming for help, *help, HELP* as cattle stirred below
until Uncle came and rescued you.

This time is not the same—
yet it seems cruel to drop onto the back
of a horse with no name, ride to a destination
we can only dream or write about,
slide from darkness into light without pen or paper.

FOSSIL FRIENDSHIP

While excavating   in the closet   I dug you up
fossil of a friend   your outline branded
onto a chip   in my memory
Retrieved accidently   you appear   on the screen
barefoot & bearded   as before   no guitar   this time
test-tubes dangling   out of your back pockets
Your friendship   an offering   I took   for granted
but not for long   I recall   all the close calls
wobbly motorcycle rides   fire towers scaled   in drugged nights
when it hardly mattered   if we breathed   tomorrow's air
Our struggles   barely a pebble   on mountain peaks   of time
whose summits   stretch   into swollen   bluesy skies
Attempts   to reach the top   always a precarious hike
a ropeless climb   bruising and scraping   our senseless pride

Lost in landscapes   of science   lost to separate states
marriages   with other mates
perhaps   you appear   to say goodbye
If these   treacherous words   fall from your lips
I will pretend   to let   you go   erase you
from the hard drive   of my mind
but in   floppy recollections   of this heart
you have left   an impression   indelibly etched
like the sensation   of a phantom limb
reminding me   of properties   beyond the physical
that cannot go   unrecognized   nor unappreciated
into a slippery present   a ceramic future   haphazard
as our glass-darkened   impressions   of God

IV KEEPER OF GOOD THINGS

HER LIPSTICK STILL ON THE CUP

A flutter of birds startled him from his sprinkling routine.
Over an hour had passed. *She should be home by now.*
He rushed by flower beds to the house, grabbed his shoes.
Which way, which way? His mind ricocheted to the trail.

He heard the low rumble of a rusted tailpipe,
saw the flash of headlights tilt away through tall grass.
Running full-blast down the Heartland Trail,
he found her half-clothed and crumpled in cattails.

Later, when the crime scene was secure,
a yellow plastic ribbon tied around the swamp,
he returned in a squad car to their empty house
where he sat and stared at the lipstick on her coffee cup.

*This morning, as usual, they brewed coffee,
listened to the thu-thump, thu-thump
of the percolator, as she read the morning paper
and he watched weather, half-heard the news.*

*When the pot stopped, she set down her paper,
laughed as pages drifted like detached wings,
made the two of them whole wheat toast with jam,
called him to the table, plates and mugs in place.*

*They ate in silence. Finches and chickadees twittered
at the feeder. She placed a napkin on his forearm,
pointed to a spot on her cheek, meaning his.
He wiped away strawberry jam and finished chewing,*

*lifted the plates to the sink where he rinsed them,
placing each one in the dishwasher. The cups could wait
for more coffee later. When he turned around,
she had gone,* to put her tennis shoes on, *he thought.*

*He hated to walk, it reminded him of training,
hours spent red-faced, sweating at the gym; he ran
and lifted weights to stay fit for law enforcement.
Retired now, he put away his gun to mow and weed.*

KEEPER OF GOOD THINGS | 45

He wished he had walked beside her today,
wished the smell of coffee had just begun to sting the air,
wished he had reached for her as she stirred from sleep
and held her to him, savoring her body heat.

SNOW GAMES

She murmured *snow*
through the thicket of my slumber
and I awoke,
and gazing from the window
saw salt licks of snow
too thin to roll into snowballs
or piece into a fort.

As children we dug tunnels,
made coffins in the snow.
We practiced death:
one lying in the ice box
cut away in deep drifts of snow,
arms folded over a flat chest
while the upright mobile one
blackened a white world,
blotting out the sun
with vast layers of snow
until the buried one screamed
into a slender thread of air
at the dark weight of cold,
at a pressing pillow of loneliness.

The one guilty of this burying
and witness to the muffled struggle,
swiftly dug out her victim's body,
saving a sister from certain doom.

Then she took a deep breath

in preparation for her turn

to practice the art of dying.

PHANTOM PET

Old and crippled with arthritis,
our Samoyed loses handfuls of white fur
before I leave on a week-long jaunt.
There was little left of her
when I returned home.
Like a white flag,
she surrendered her simple will
to the complexity of our lives,
filled the sameness
of everyday skies
with fluffy impressions.

Yesterday marked a week
since her body stiffened
against its final breath.
At fourteen, the steps
were mountain treachery,
too steep for her to climb.
Her front paws were cracked and bled.
She slept often, a sprawled snowbank
drifting through our den and hallway.

Almost losing track of her,
like dog food bagged and closeted,
I wrap my arms around her memory,
recall those scrambled eggs
I fed her against house rules.
Winter's toasted almond eyes
and high-pitched dolphin whine
pleaded for that final forbidden treat.
I leaned against the porch doorway
as she gently gobbled
the softness of their yellow warmth
like swallowed sunlight.

Tonight I expect to hear her snuffling
as I spray leftovers from dinner dishes.
I can't shake her off
while her ghost hairs still cling
to the backyard gate.

THE GREAT LAKE SUPERIOR'S REIGN

Lake Superior, the deepest of the Great Lakes
and largest body of fresh water in the world,
is known as "the graveyard of ships."

Blue-blood of Five Jewels, this chic sapphire
cool as North's Pole, pools over great distance.
When the surface is smooth, waters run deep,
leave clues on tangled fathomless bottom
remnants of dangerous depths, sneaky storms.
Oblivious to Superior's strength,

men become victims of that liquid strength
hidden in glint carats of a sapphire
surface, disappear in waves of her storms.
Too late they spyglass the rock-cliff's distance,
panic as their ships sink to the bottom
soundlessly, a water sleep in her deep

forever. More than one thousand feet deep,
this fluid body holds no solid strength.
Sleekness bends to soft sand at the bottom
where *Edmund Fitzgerald* smudges sapphire
clarity. Light dies—rays measure distance,
disperse far from the bloodshot eyes of storms.

As hosts of unclaimed ghosts stir their own storms,
ships settle in mystified silence, deep
in reverie, safe and snug, a distance
from topside fury, stuck in silt-smoothed strength.
Surface waves like jagged shards of sapphire
dissolve in foam, never reach the bottom.

Schooners, cargo ships trim the lake's bottom,
feed the growling hunger of savage storms
where onyx murk replaces sky, sapphire
waters. Tugboats, cruise ships, schooners pulled deep
into the bowels of turbulent strength
where treasures rest at a deep-sixed distance.

Superior stills. Each beached fleet's distance
stretches along an eternal bottom
of what ifs, dashed to bits by noble strength.

This sovereign exudes royal crowns of storms,
ruling the surface while sailors dive deep,
undertowed in the lake's inky sapphire.

Deceived by the distance of regal storms,
men and boats line the bottom of this deep
sky, its upside-down strength: a star sapphire.

LESSON UNDER GLASS

The sign reads: $14.93 per pound
above the Plexiglas-sided tank
whose top and bottom are lopped off
of this miniature globe standing
in the middle of the produce department
at our local Wal-Mart.

At first I don't see them. I must look down
to notice a captured community of lobsters.
Some lie in shock, statue-still at the bottom
of the pool, their tails curled under armored bodies
while larger, more pushy crustaceans
scurry along the backs of fellow captives.
Their faces sharp as swords, these bullies
lunge at one another, shoving first one,
then another, backwards, in this sterile space
which is all that is left of their ocean.

I walk closer, look down into bubbly water,
note futility in the rubber-banding of their claws.
I lean toward a heavy one,
look into his black bead of an eye,
say slowly, "You, sir, are a goner."
He moves away, legs akimbo,
feelers twitching,
his little orange facial spikes
sharp with disdain.

I want to scold this lobster-lot,
convince them to stop shoving, quit fighting.
Like a prophet, I want to warn them
of their future: a real and imminent battle,
one final plunge none can possibly survive.

MINDLESS CLUTTER OF SKY JUNK

Junk's afloat in our atmosphere,
its far-flung, far-out orbit seems
right now and here, a bit obscure.

I thought that space was emptiness
peppered with a few planets,
malted moons, a sun sizzling
while translucent shakes of stars
eddy the galaxy.

Spent rocket boosters loosed
from stronger gravity orbit the earth.
Inertia keeps ellipse winding around,
frenetic as a gong about to break.

My mind, twisting through tubules,
thought there were places where
footloose mentality roamed free,
Wyoming range for bison ideas—
a band-aid strip of galaxy,
flattened out endlessly, undisturbed.

We've rudely interrupted space
with our crude atmospheric junk.
We've mucked the natural freedom
of its ways, to shun forevermore,
or nudge away the tracked display
of man's material mortality.

This vast trash can of sky,
more than 8500 objects deep,
has warped my sense of space.

WE TALK GERMS
IN ALATEEN GROUP

At first I try to explain what they do,
not what they are. I read the warning
from our school nurse about whooping cough,
how we pass the invisible through close contact,
cozying next to each other in class,
chewing each other's pencils.

I describe the symptoms:
coughing fits that turn lips blue,
coughing until you throw up,
growing weaker after weeks of this
incessant coughing, coughing.

We discuss how to prevent
this insidious spread of germs:
cover the cough with an elbow
or a tissue, never the palm of a hand,
wash hands often with soap and water,
stay home when feeling sick,
see a doctor if symptoms persist,
take antibiotics, then wait for five days
before returning to school,
no longer contagious.

I push the Kleenex box across the table
toward muffled sounds of a student's sniffles.
"I think I've already got it," she says.
"Me, too," chimes another, swiping his nose.
We talk germs. I give advice
they probably will not take,
or will take only in the throes of a crisis,
spreading an unforeseen enemy like wildfire,
like this disease of addiction
for which there is no cure.

THINKING OF CROOKSTON

>Dru Sjodin's body was found near Crookston, MN
>in April 2004, five months after she was abducted
>from a mall parking lot in Grand Forks, ND.

Something sweeter brought
his family here, to the Red River Valley,
to this small town whose name
was decided by a coin toss.
For fifteen years they migrated
from Texas, picking sugar beets
farmers hauled by truckloads each fall
to the American Crystal Sugar Company.
Finally they moved here for good.

~

In ninth grade, he dropped
out of school and worked at the plant
until he turned his back on sweetness.
He turned violent in this green river town
where the Red Lake River oxbows
through the heart of Crookston;
did his time, and time again,
returning like a terrible flood
no one wanted to recall,
to its ravine and twisting river.

~

A few months out of the slammer
something new and sweet drew him
to Grand Forks, to the mall,
to a lingerie shop where silky scents
and shiny undergarments tantalized him.
And when the blonde clerk asked him
did he need any help, her lips looked sticky
as a lollipop that had just been licked,
then set aside for later. After that
he called and listened to her say again,
"May I help you?" and he thought
of lips as round and full as Tootsie pops.

~

One fall day after work, her ear to her cell phone
and a boyfriend's voice on the other end,
he took her at knife point, pushed her into his car
parked near hers in the mall parking lot.
Then he stole from her what he could
and tried to squeeze the honey from her heart
until she no longer breathed this earth's air,
but her spirit escaped him as he could not
escape his festering soul, the death sentence.

KEEPER OF EVERY GOOD THING

Ready to move, I empty file cabinets
and drawers, wheel in a trash can
where it looms smack dab in the middle
of the room, lest I forget my mission.
I give away all the candy—black licorice
for the boss, *Dove* chocolates wrapped
in tinfoil messages for the girls,
hard candies for our company jar.

                I tackle green
hanging files, divest myself of papers
too faded or grainy to read.
I march private stuff straight to the shredder,
shed books, tapes, three-ring binders,
in-service training folders, scribbled-in notebooks.
I save every paper clip that isn't tarnished,
my *Jonathan Livingston Seagull* paperweight,
a cat-shaped gum holder. I drift
to the cafeteria for a cup of coffee.

Two weeks later, with boxes
still on the credenza and time to kill,
I drag the same brown trash receptacle
from the closet, refill its huge empty gut
with a colorful assortment of flyers
and brochures accumulated
for more than seventeen years.

                    When done purging,
I have that just-finished-with-a-haircut feeling
after stray hairs are brushed from my neck,
lighter by a long-shot. Then I flash
to a time, not long ago, when I found
my Red Cross Swimmer's card
while cleaning out my parents' house.
I tossed the thing, having not missed it
for over fifty years, unless perchance,
I might have traded it in
for a ticket to eternity.

DELIBERATE DAY

For once the day did not wrestle
me into a choke hold as the soles
of my feet touched the bedroom carpet.
For once I hit the snooze alarm,
not an alarming number of times,
just twice, two four-minute intervals,
then I untangled from the sheets.
I rose like a fiddlestick fern unraveling,
like corn stalks slashing their salute to the sky.

My feet carried me toward the bathroom
then I fed the dogs, herding them
into the backyard. I ate a banana, drank water.
I dressed, took my walking sticks for a spin
on an asphalt trail that parted a sea of wild flowers—
a path grosgrained by tree shadows, ribboning
through green and more green, field and forest.
When I returned, I showered,
blended a blueberry protein shake,
swallowed a fistful of vitamins.

For once I did not ricochet off the walls,
glancing at the kitchen clock, checking my watch
to see when I needed to zoom from the house.
For once I thought: *This is the life I chose.*
Like a wild rose, I can sink my roots anywhere.
Today I choose to bloom here.

V CAST ON / CAST OFF

RODIN'S *THE THINKER* (1880)

What could he have been thinking
sitting naked and alone upon a rock?
Was he so wrapped up in newness of thought
that even watching an unprotected back
didn't matter? Perhaps a jagged jolt
as electrifying as lightning entered his brain;
a spark hit his mind-forest like wildfire
baring the leftover landscape in sooty silence.

Or did he watch an ant drag
its burden through dust
while bronze-gleamed sunlight reflected
in star-spokes on a hypnotic black back?
Stripped of clothes, of self-consciousness,
unaroused by woman-passion,
a man ponders his place
in space and time
not in words, but in divisions
that separate him from other living things.

He sees how his arms bear skin and hair,
no bark or fur to keep him warm on winter nights.
His fingers and hands grasp and carry,
caress his woman and child, wield clubs,
build traps, mold pots, gather seeds, seek shelter.
Watching his chest, he sees a heart pound
in rhythm to ancestral drumbeats
celebrating birth, death, battle, the hunt.
His feet carry him. He walks upright.

His mind opens like a book,
to first pages; a prelude to the story
which will unfold like a bear rug
before a bright cave fire,
warming and softening uneven ground.
From this crude seat, his life travels
like a spear thrust into history
as he remembers, in stick-figure images
scratched upon mind-walls,
as he slowly explores
an uninhabited cave
of his own creation.

CAST ON / CAST OFF

I did cast my fate upon you
O genie of a leg lamp, I intoned,
make me whole again,
mend my foot, the fifth metatarsal,
a dancer's break, broken when I wasn't dancing.
You delivered.

Now the doctor says I no longer need you.
Removable. Perhaps recyclable? I ask. Headshake, no.
Do I hand your scuffed remains over to the clinic staff,
or throw you, old strappy shell,
into the nearest trash bin? No.
I carry you like a gray baby to my car,
set you gently on the seat,
and take your picture.

For six weeks we slept together.
I washed you, wore you.
In my brokenness you clutched me.
I cursed you and my klutziness.
Ineptitude became my fashion statement.

Four days have passed since I strapped you
into my car, a permanent backseat passenger.
You blend well with the current decor.
One day, when looking through my rear view mirror
and seeing you, unattached and off-duty,
you will become a crippling reminder
butting up against my joy
of having two good feet.

When I give you the boot,
the heave-ho, Boot-O,
I hope you understand why
I held you hostage for so long.
I became as attached to you
as you were to me.

BICYCLING HIGHWAY 65

Twice I two-wheeled it through Cambridge,
once above my own bicycle pedals,
another time on the back of a Santana tandem,
bobbing to the time of piston legs in front of me.

Sometimes the only thing a tired bicyclist considers
is the sun's heat settling on asphalt and skin,
a dryness drawing attention to the phlegmy throat,
or panting that sounds like someone in hot pursuit

of you—only it is you—your chest heaving,
working its way into a breathing rhythm
until you squint, wishing the water tower closer
so you can stop, stretch, stand—ride on.

On to something else smaller, growing larger,
as you pass pastures with numbered street signs, you
get giddy, wonder if cows receive mail along this road,
this suburb of a town you plan to soon wheel through.

RENDERED PEACHLESS

On the tray table in back of me,
a peach once nestled in paper towel.
When I finished working, I planned to savor it.
My mouth puckered with the imagined sensation
of peach skin like the velvety lips of horses,
the juicy flesh tempered with a tart sweetness
found only in perfectly ripe peaches,
that bruiseless and unblemished fruit
picked with dainty delicacy—
perhaps while wearing white gloves—
then wrapped and packed with considerate care.

I could sleep with this peach,
roll it over my bare body,
fill my pores with the succulent aroma of fresh peach.
I could squeeze pink juice into the cup of my bellybutton,
fondle this fruit,
peel the skin from its soft body.
I would nibble its flesh—slowly, at first,
then with harder, bigger bites; let the juices flow,
a sticky waterfall over my chin, onto my breasts.

I could devour all the flesh, or so I thought,
until my daughter breezes in from her job,
smelling of french fries and burgers.
"Oh, that looks *soooo* good."
I don't need to ask what she means.
I have already dreamed my fill of this fruit.

Feeling weak, I say, "Go ahead, you can have it."
I hold it out to her. My hand trembles. "It's still cool."
I admire how it nestles in my hand
like a newborn baby's head.
I hand her the orb, devoid of my fantasies.
She changes clothes, leaves for the race track,
never tells me if her peach was as juicy as mine.

TOMATO SPECULATION

In the land of more-than-plenty, there's a shortage of tomatoes. Their prices are high, their quality marginal. So, no tomatoes (no small potatoes in my book) if I grasp the email from the dietary department correctly. It takes a hospital to inform you of your salad's anemic condition. A tight market, I read. Over-ripe and bursting its thin red skin. The report from growing regions draws dreary pictures of Hurricane Wilma's rage in Immokalee, Florida, twirling tomatoes into bloody pulp. The Sunshine State's Quincy and Palmetto tomato harvest is finished, fields brown, nothing doing or growing, until June and May, respectively. Mexico's crop plight lost to blight. Freeze warnings in Florida keep our salads fruitless. We fill the gap with cucumbers and olives, one or two Vidalia onion slices. We forget we ever really liked tomatoes. Perhaps the rumor is true: we would have lived forever without them; they always were the forbidden fruit.

BANANAMANIA

Inspired by Top Banana artist, Renie Breskin Adams

If I were a banana—
I would be yellow from ear to ear & head to toe.
I would be boneless, squishy & full of myself.
I would have a sunny disposition.
I would glow with my own warm mellowness.

If *I* were a banana—
I would be photogenic (especially when lying on one side).
Crescent moons & I could identify.
I would be tickled by tarantulas, have nightmares about hungry monkeys & empty crates.
Yellow Submarine & Donovan's *Mellow Yellow* would be *my* theme songs.

If I *were* a banana—
I would admire the swell shapes of parentheses, fermatas, hammocks, rubber schoolyard swings & pointed toe shoes.
I would fill the mouths of hungry people.
I would worship the sun.
I would have a natural affinity for corn, highlighters, lemons, dandelions & certain polka dot bikinis.

If I were a *ripe* banana—
no one could make me green with envy.
I would never be blue.
I would not see red.
When I became black-peeled,
I could dole myself out for baking & suntan lotions.

If I were a *banana*—
I would extol the virtues of bile & ragweed.
I would be brazen as a brass band.
I would prize the slipperiness of butter & margarine.
Being fruity, I would fling my perfume like a boomerang.
I would be the best banana in the bunch.
I would live as though the sun had already risen on tomorrow.

DANCER EYES

for Maxine

She dances with her eyes:
copper pennies bright
glow incandescent
embers deep inside.
She dances with her eyes,
her legs a blur
in jigs of time,
Woman of Infinite Steps
yet to be danced.
She dances with her eyes—
her face a map:
its furrowed topographic blend
a blessed ballroom
of missteps and midnight trysts.
She dances with her eyes.
I catch the glint.
It carries me
so near the flame
I think I'll crisp
to ash, yet crave
the twirling heat
that never fades
from fiery eyes.
She dances with her eyes.
I must follow her.
For where she dances
I can only venture
with a partner
who dances footloose
into blackest nights,
who shoulders vibrant messages
far beyond the blistering stars.

BIRTHPLACE OF A POET

Like a Wyoming tumbleweed,
I twisted from the womb,
became a child of the wind.

I tumbled to the Midwest,
to Minnesota, my parents' birthplace,
where Lake Superior became my mirror.

When I grew, we moved and I took a piece
of her liquid beauty with me, a sliver of blue
riding the waves of my memory.

I became a child of the forest, the pines—
red pines, Norway pines, scruffy Jack pines,
the orange, fallen needles prickly under my feet.

Still a tumbleweed by nature, I traveled among
stripes of asphalt rivers, Interstate highways
connecting suburbs and cities. I became a bramble

in the bushes of urban life—dancing to reggae music
in streets overlooking the freeway, my body swaying
like the tops of trees I'd climbed, whose sap I wore

like a badge of childhood quests to reach the sky.
I shaped myself into ways others dreamed me.
Tumbling along a path against my nature, I stumbled

upon words. Words tumble anywhere—no one owns them,
not even the wind. Words form any shape, or sound.
They can go where you go, where you've been, or will be.

Words became my tumbleweed path, my western nature
braided in a blend of European roots and galactic thought,
poured out on the page like a big dipper of Northern Lights.

ABOUT THE AUTHOR

Charmaine Pappas Donovan, recent president of the League of Minnesota Poets, has prose and poetry published in various newspapers, magazines, journals and anthologies. As project manager for *County Lines*, a Minnesota sesquicentennial publication showcasing the poetry of 120 Minnesota poets, she also co-edited the anthology. She lives in rural Brainerd, Minnesota and Reed Point, Montana with her husband and pet menagerie. This is her first collection.

Lost Hills Books
www.losthillsbks.com